Argentina
Coloring The World

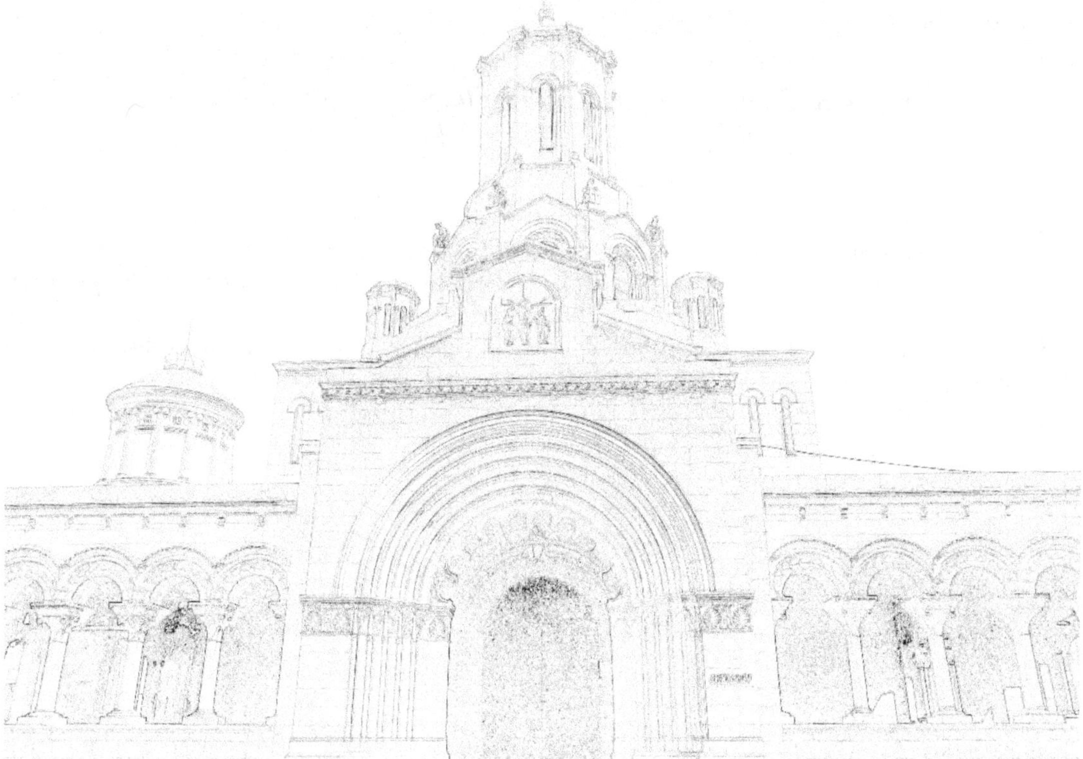

Anthony Hutzler

Sketch Coloring Book

Copyright: Published in the United States by Anthony Hutzler
Published July 2016

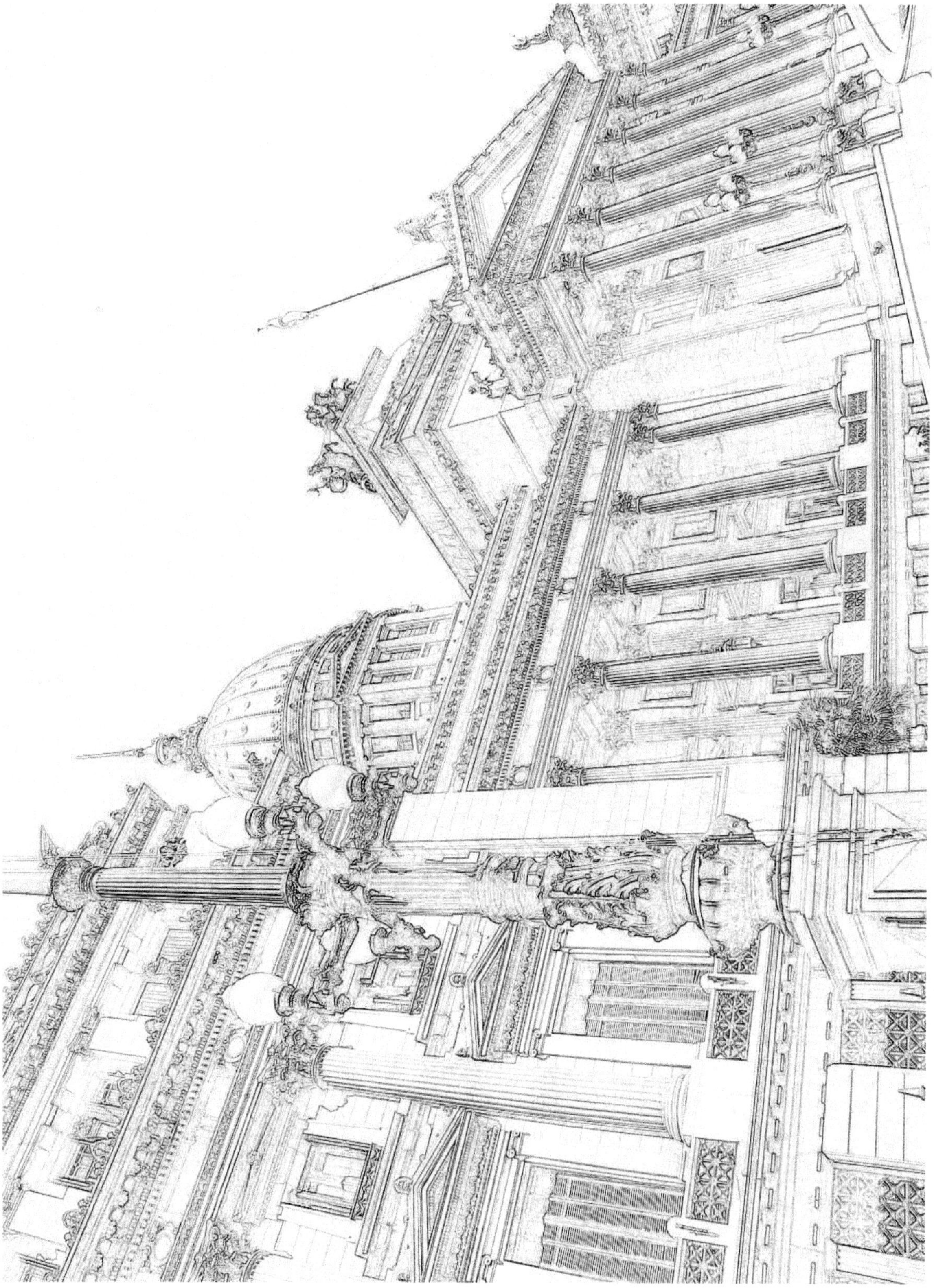

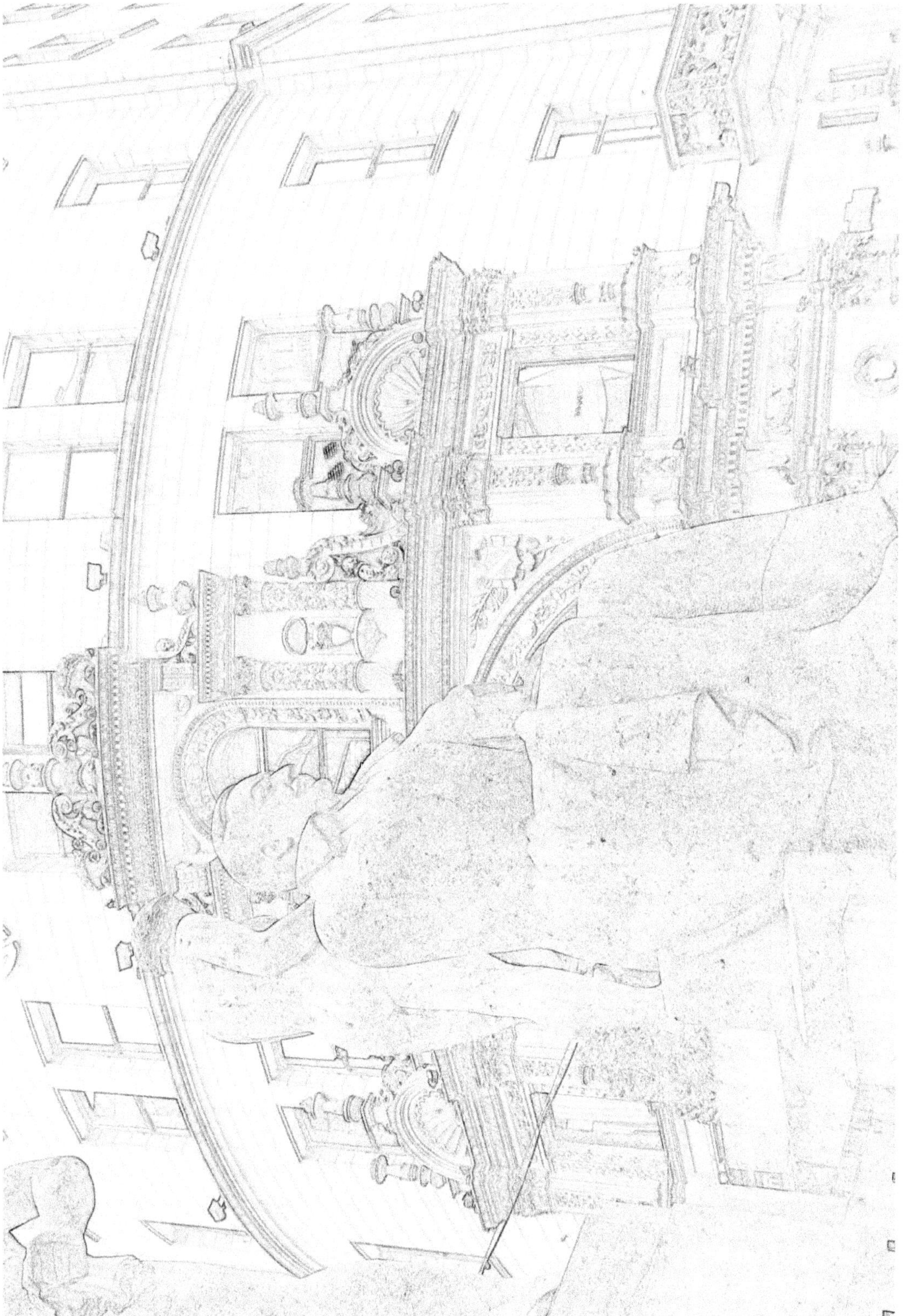

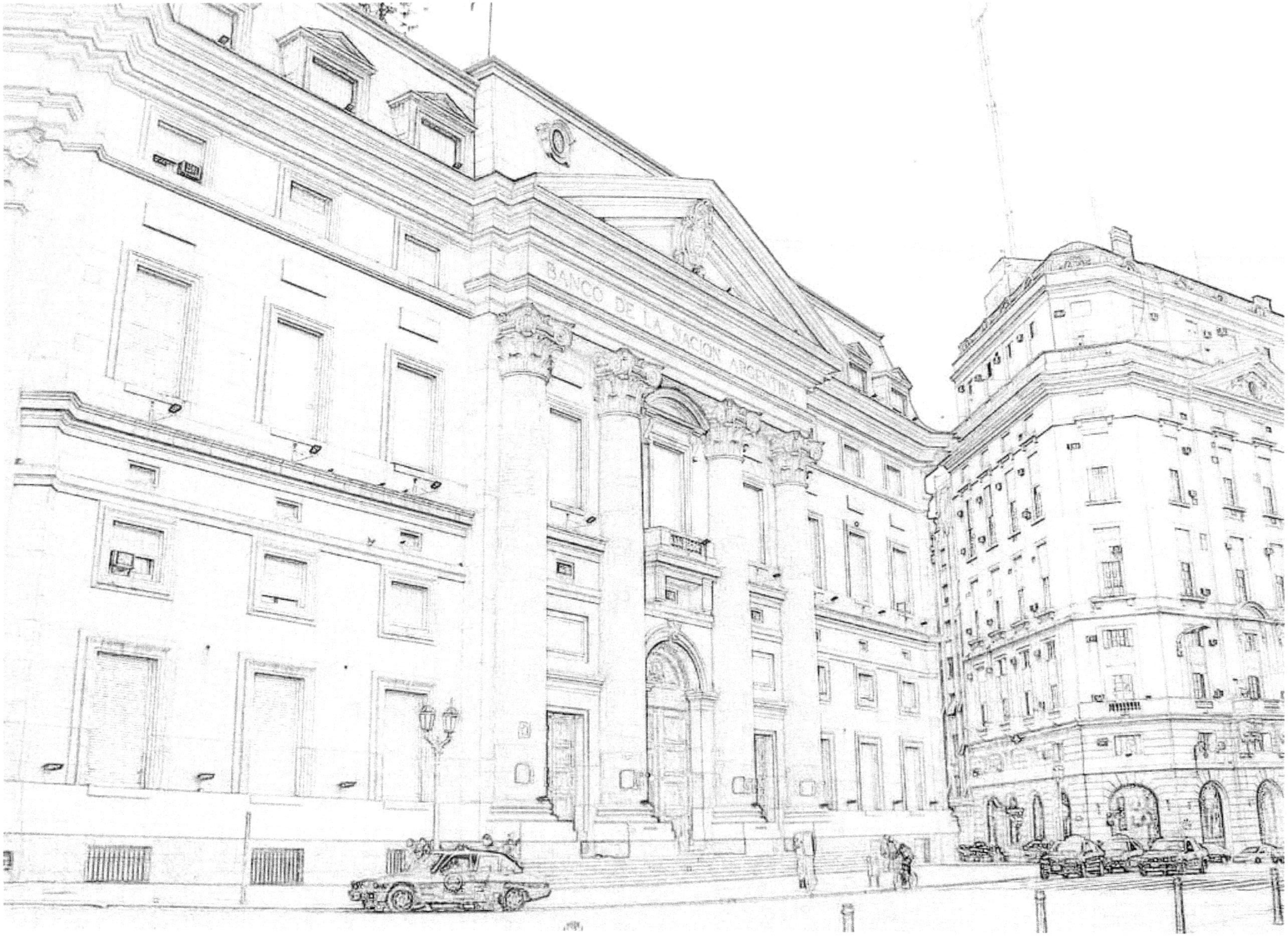
BANCO DE LA NACION ARGENTINA

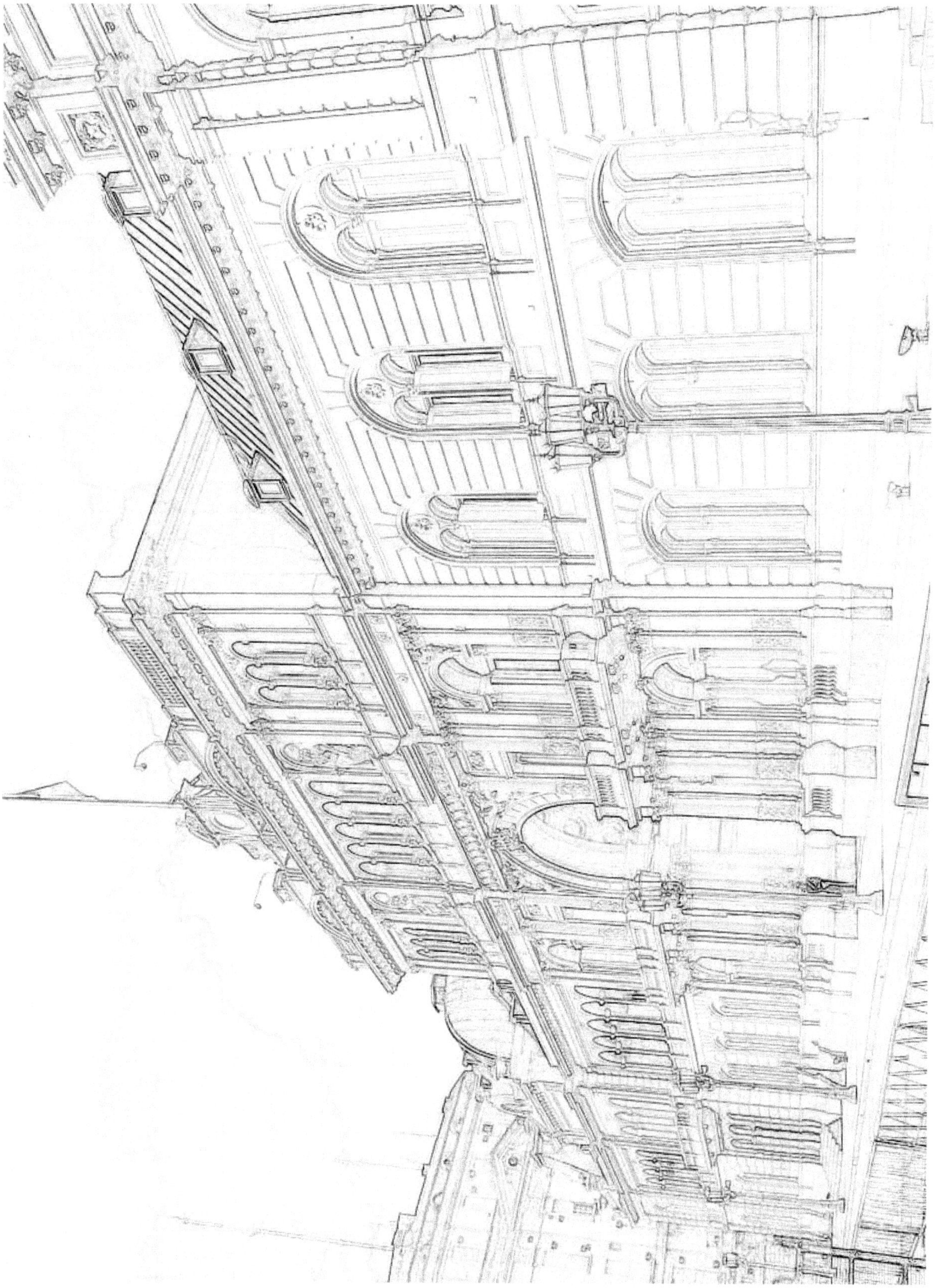

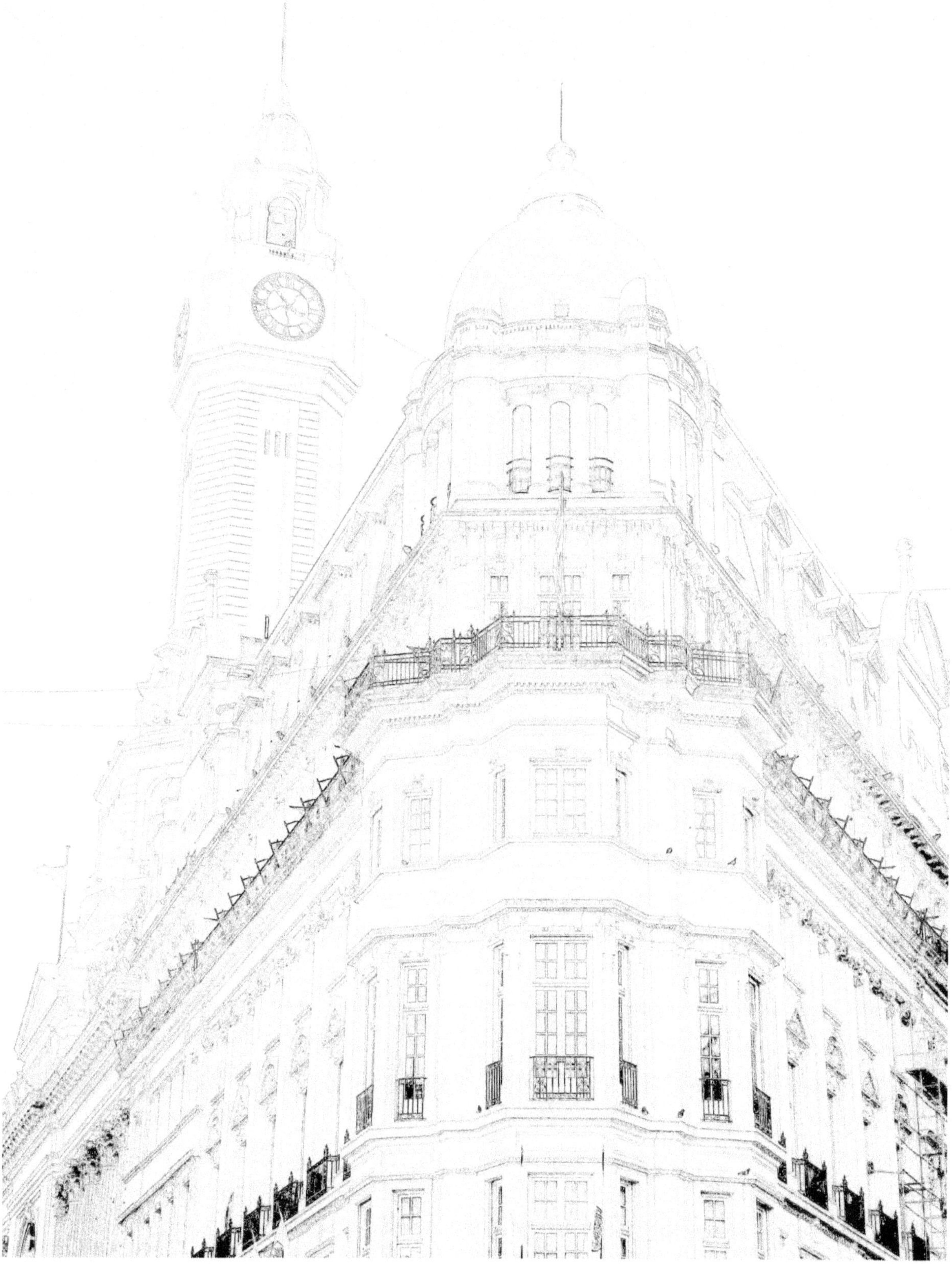

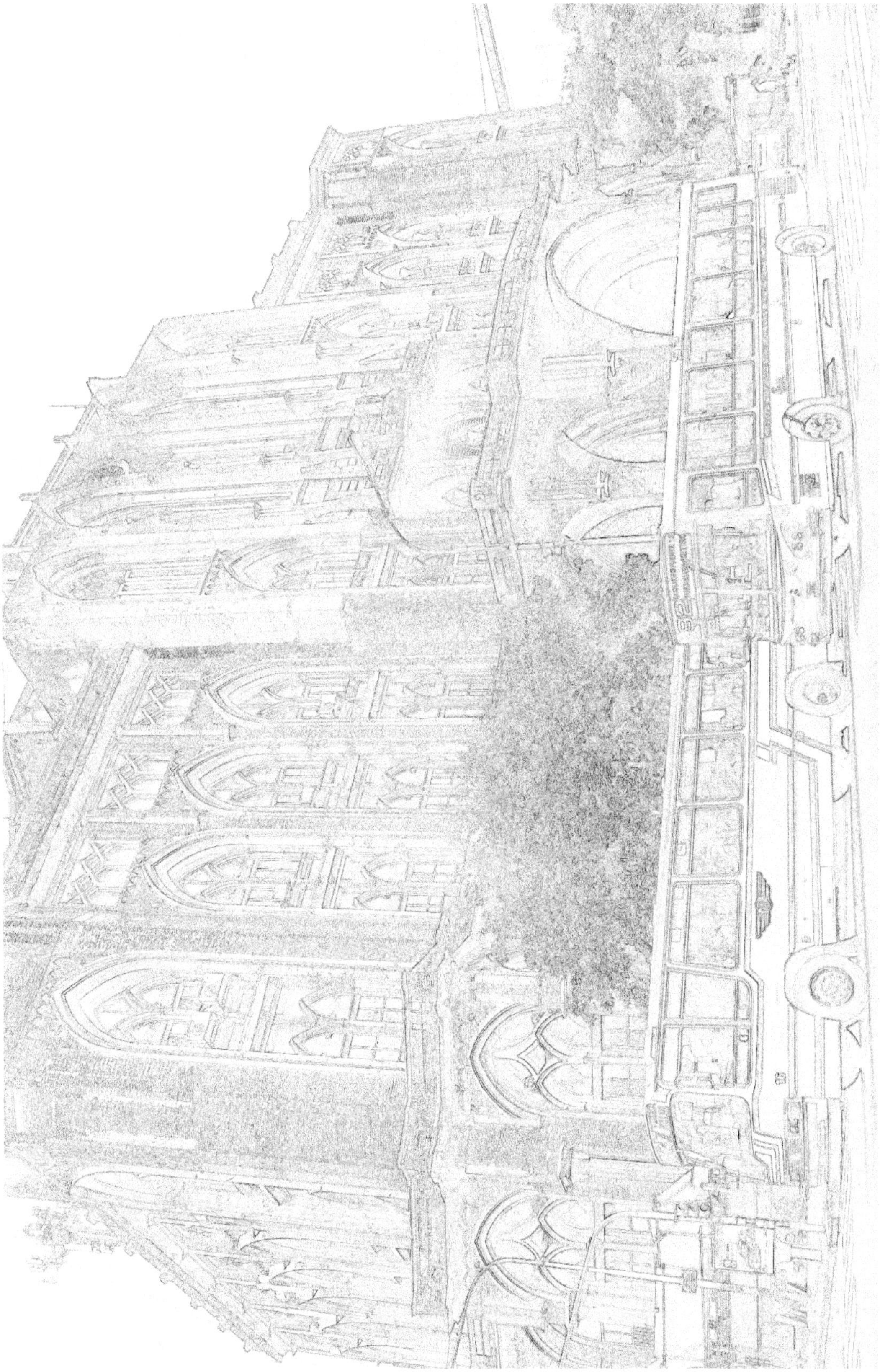

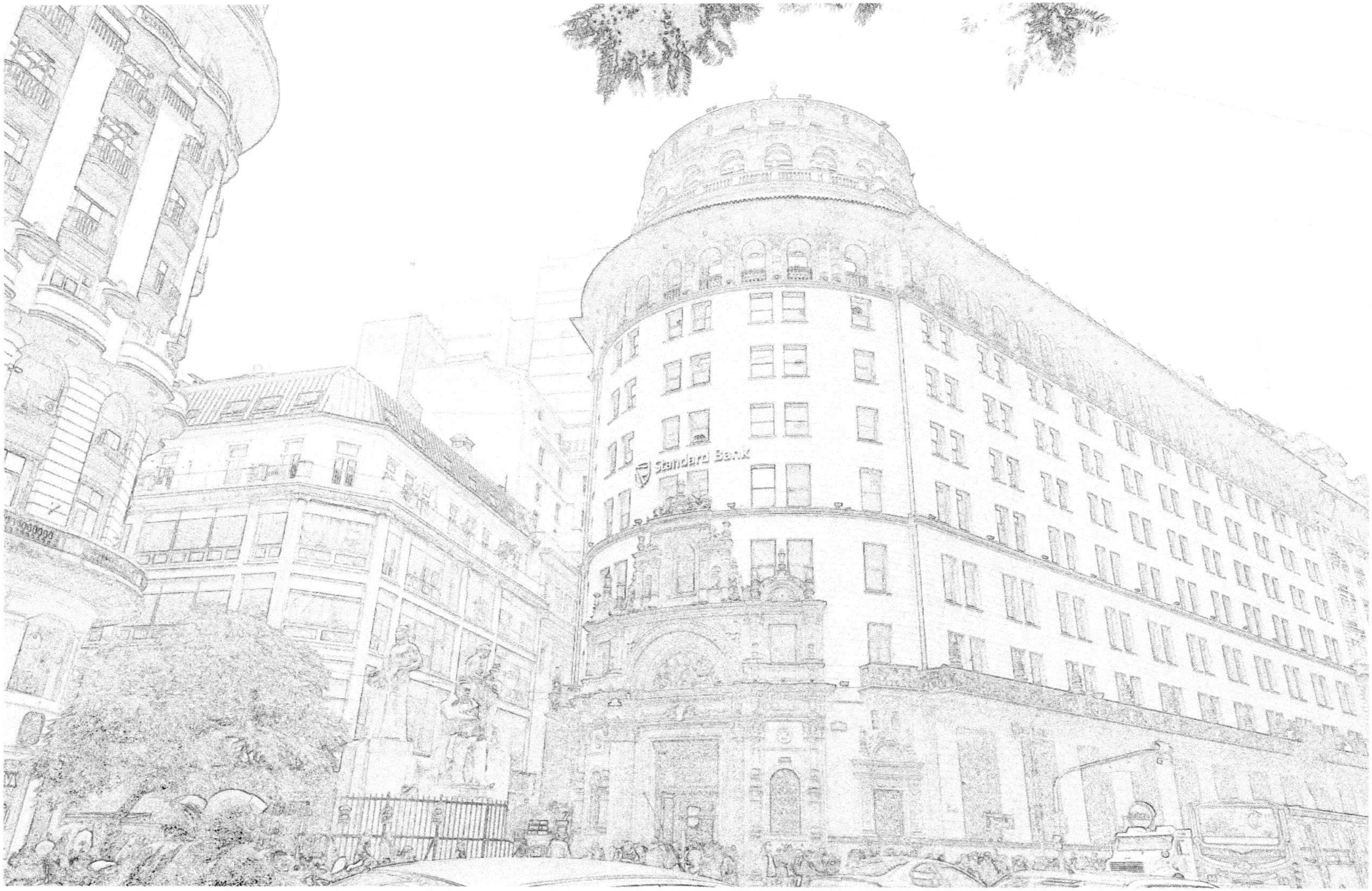
Standard Bank

BANCO DE LA NACION ARGENTINA

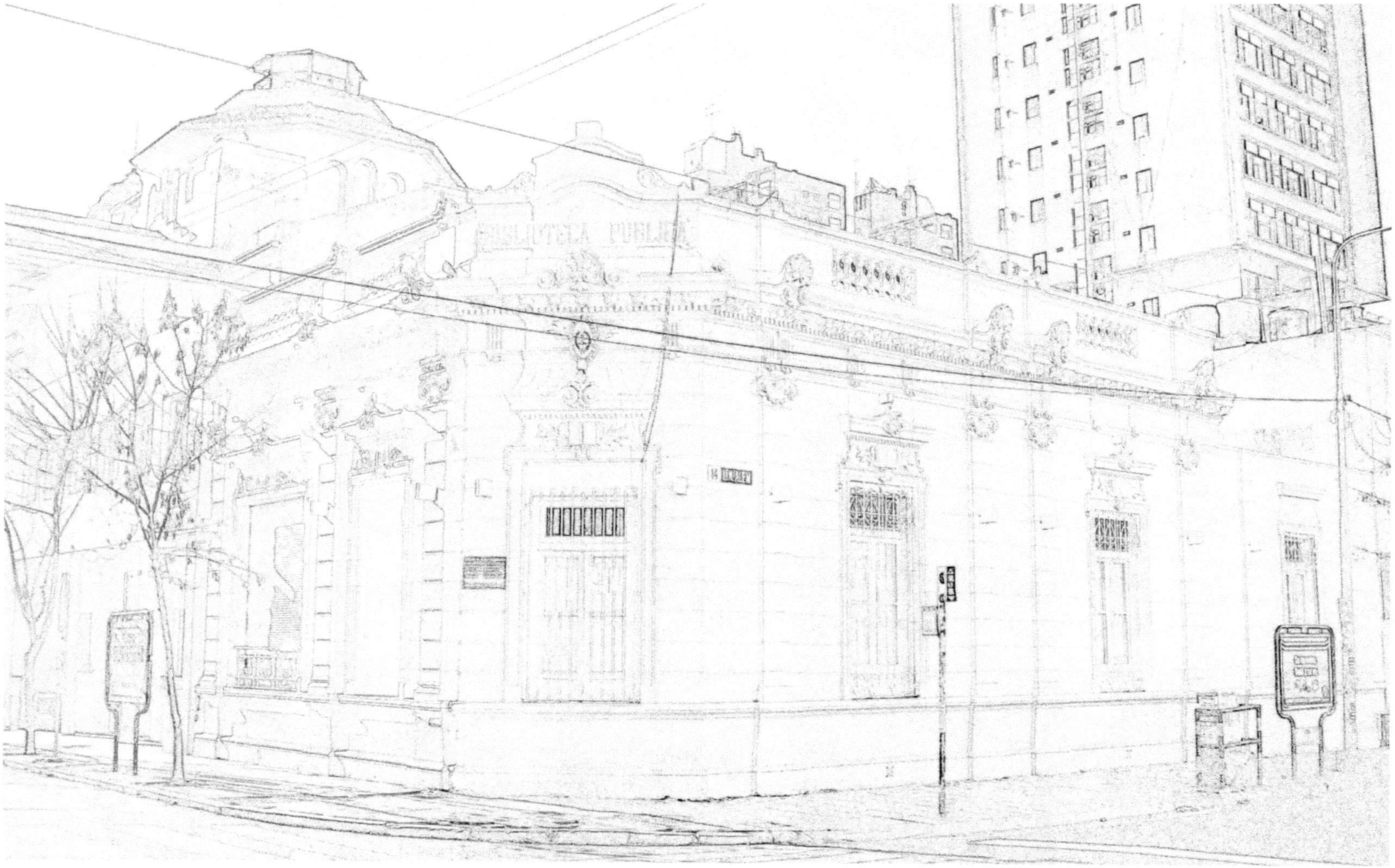
BIBLIOTECA PUBLICA

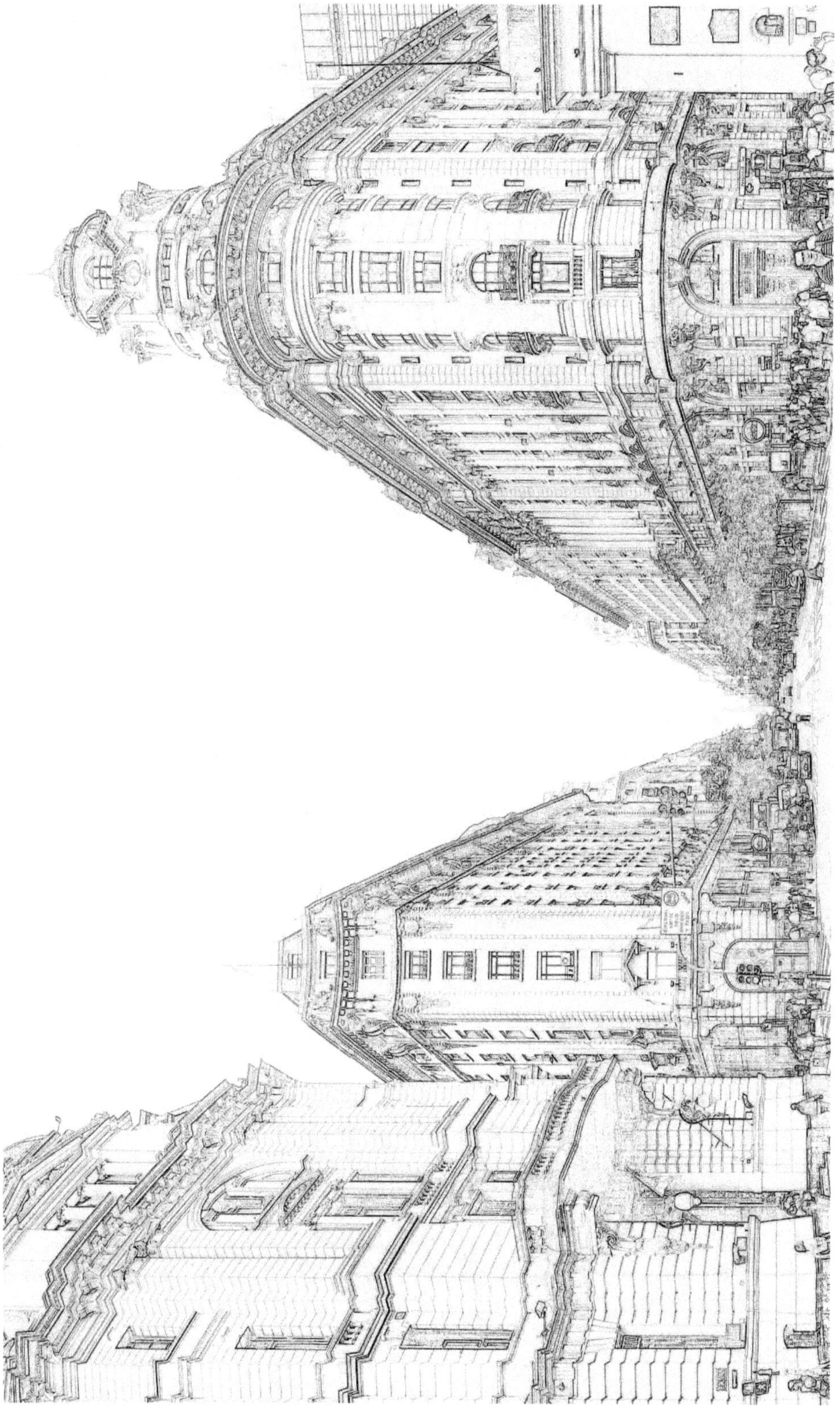

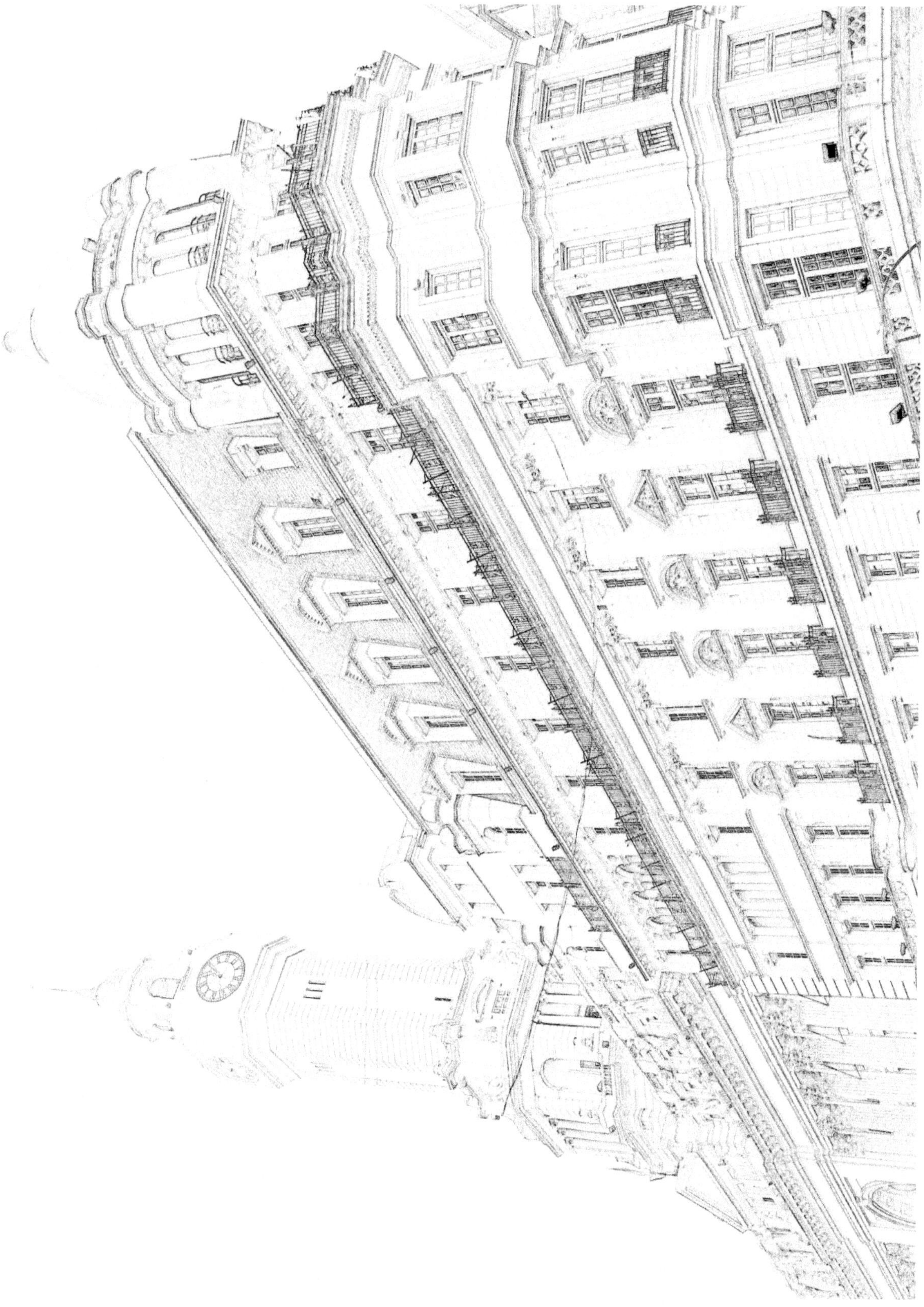

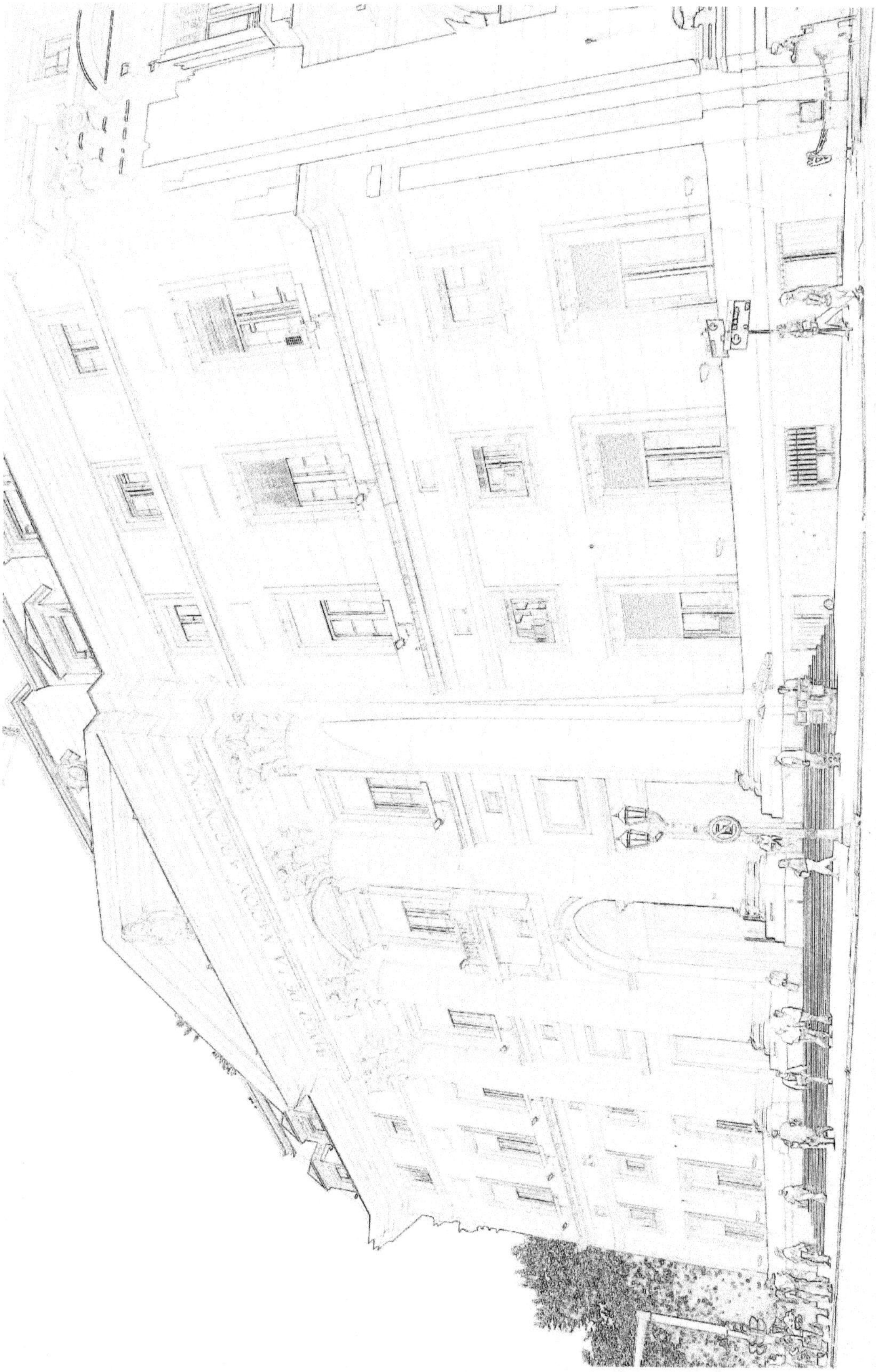

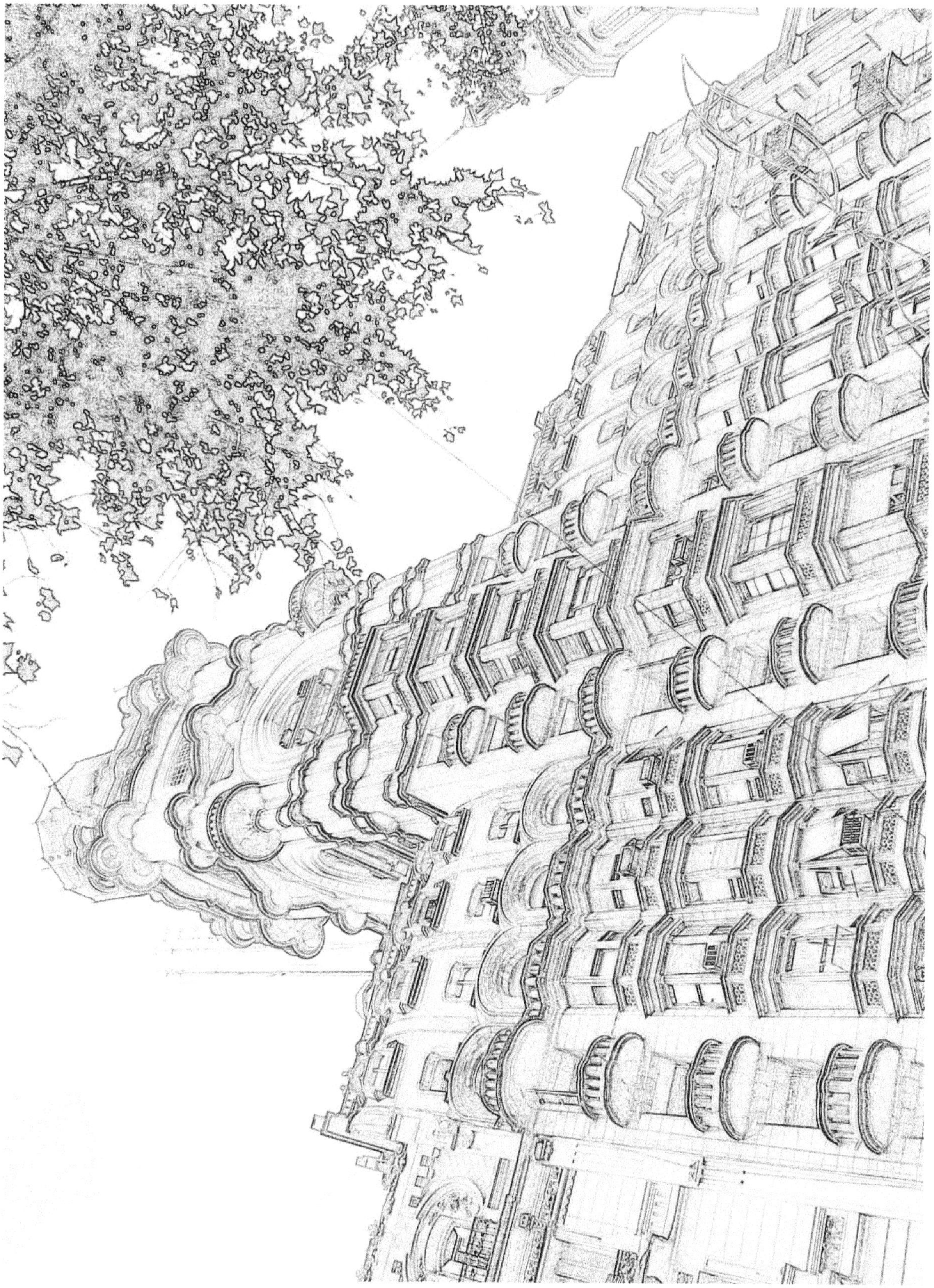

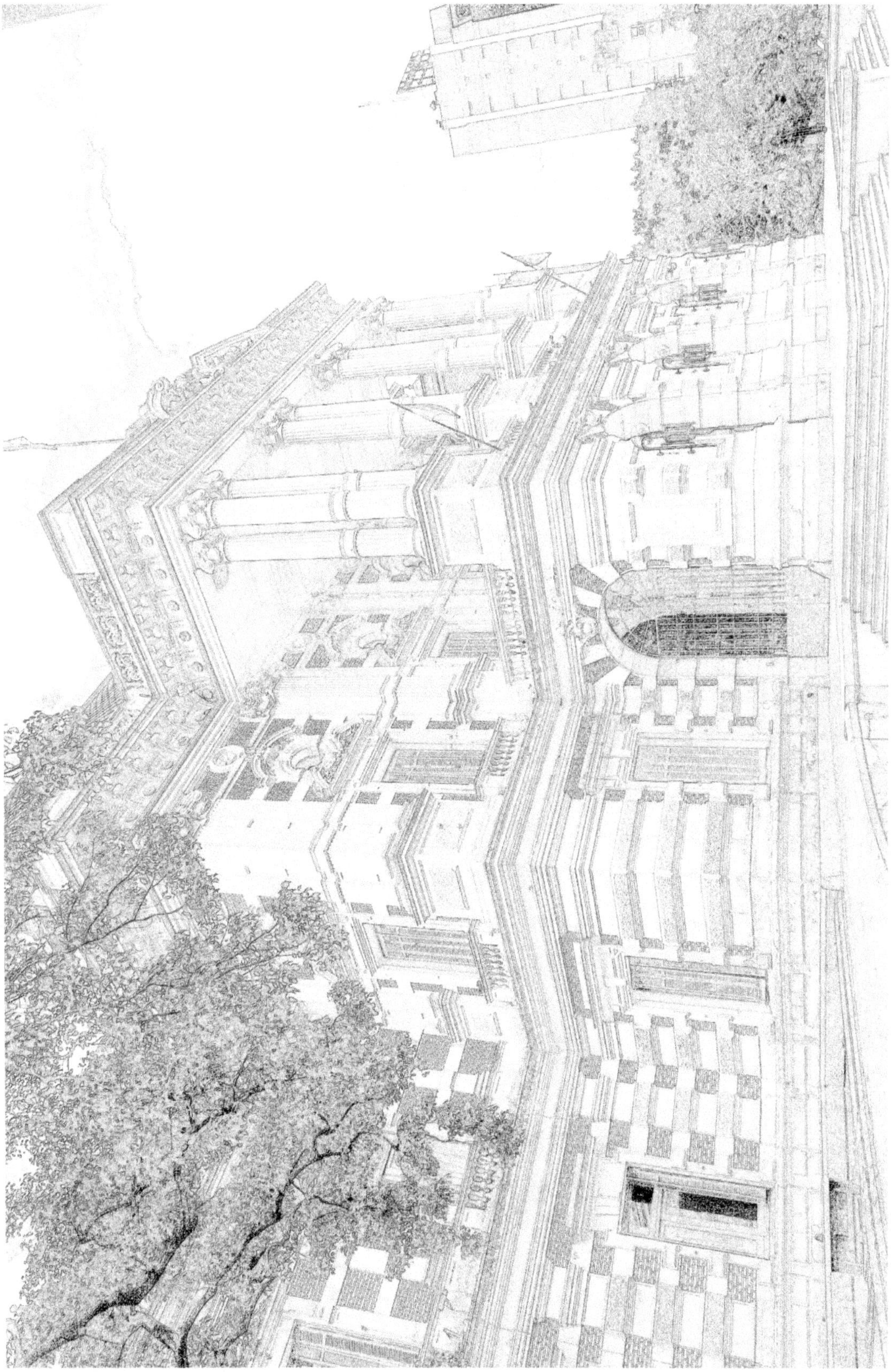

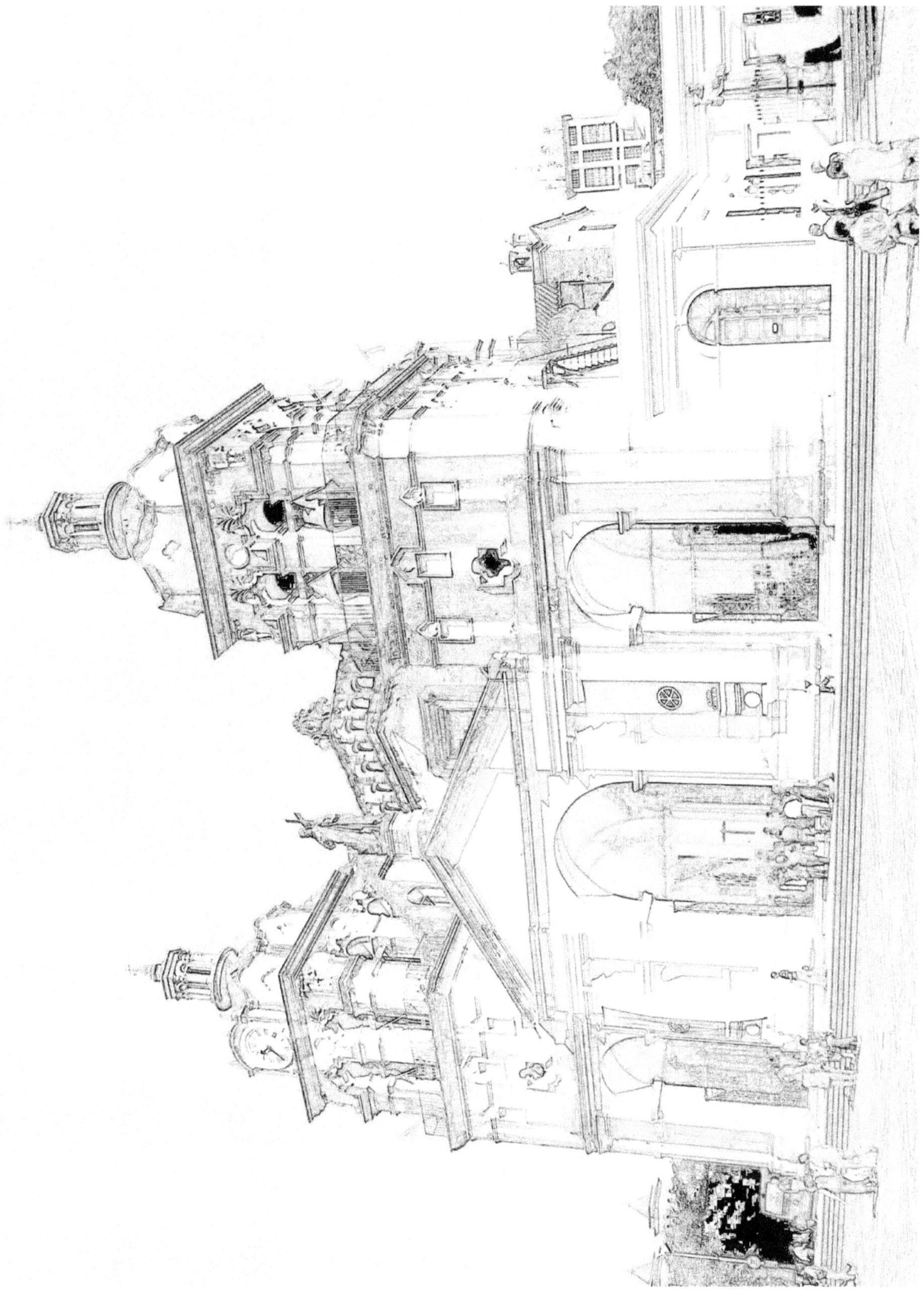

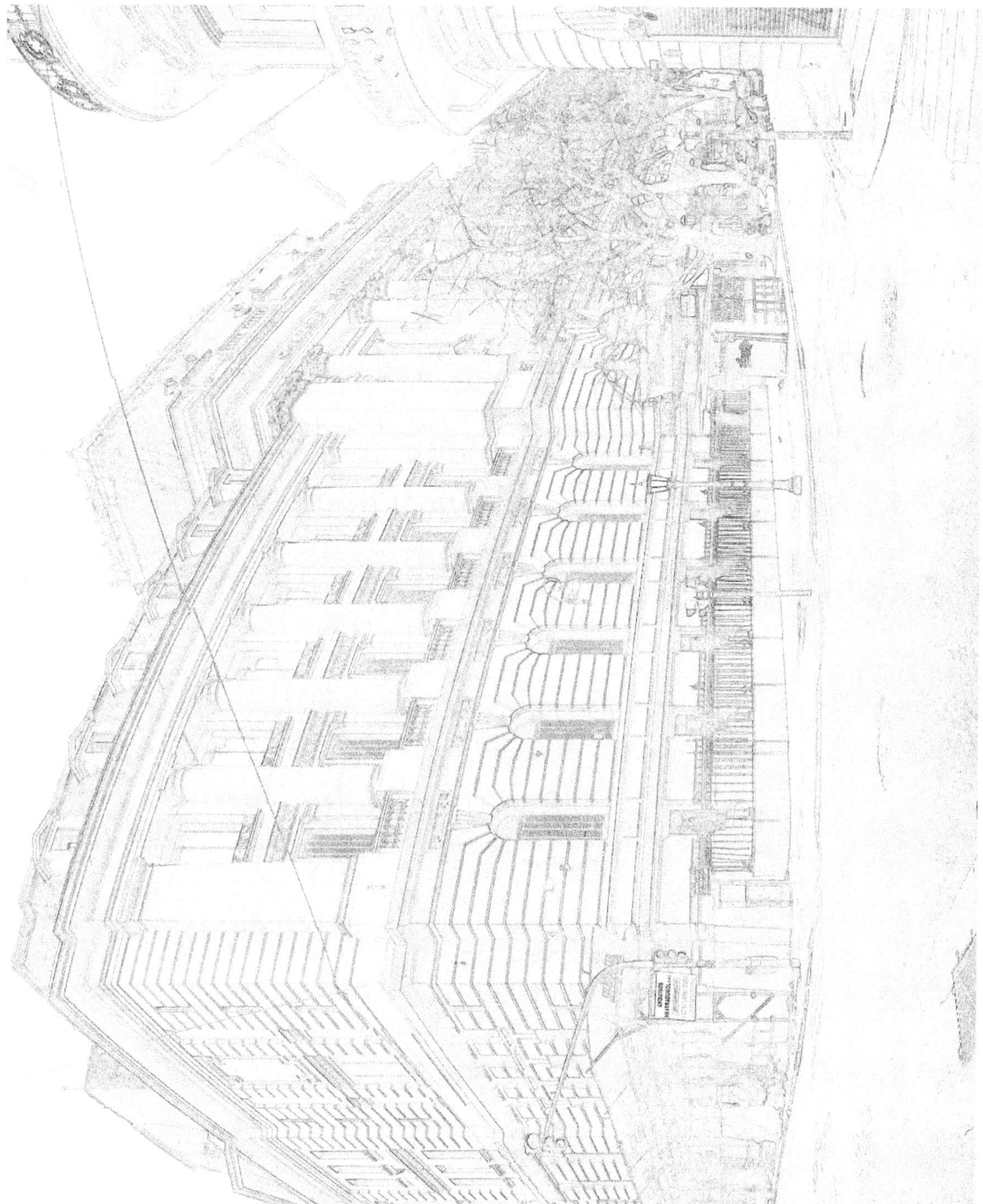

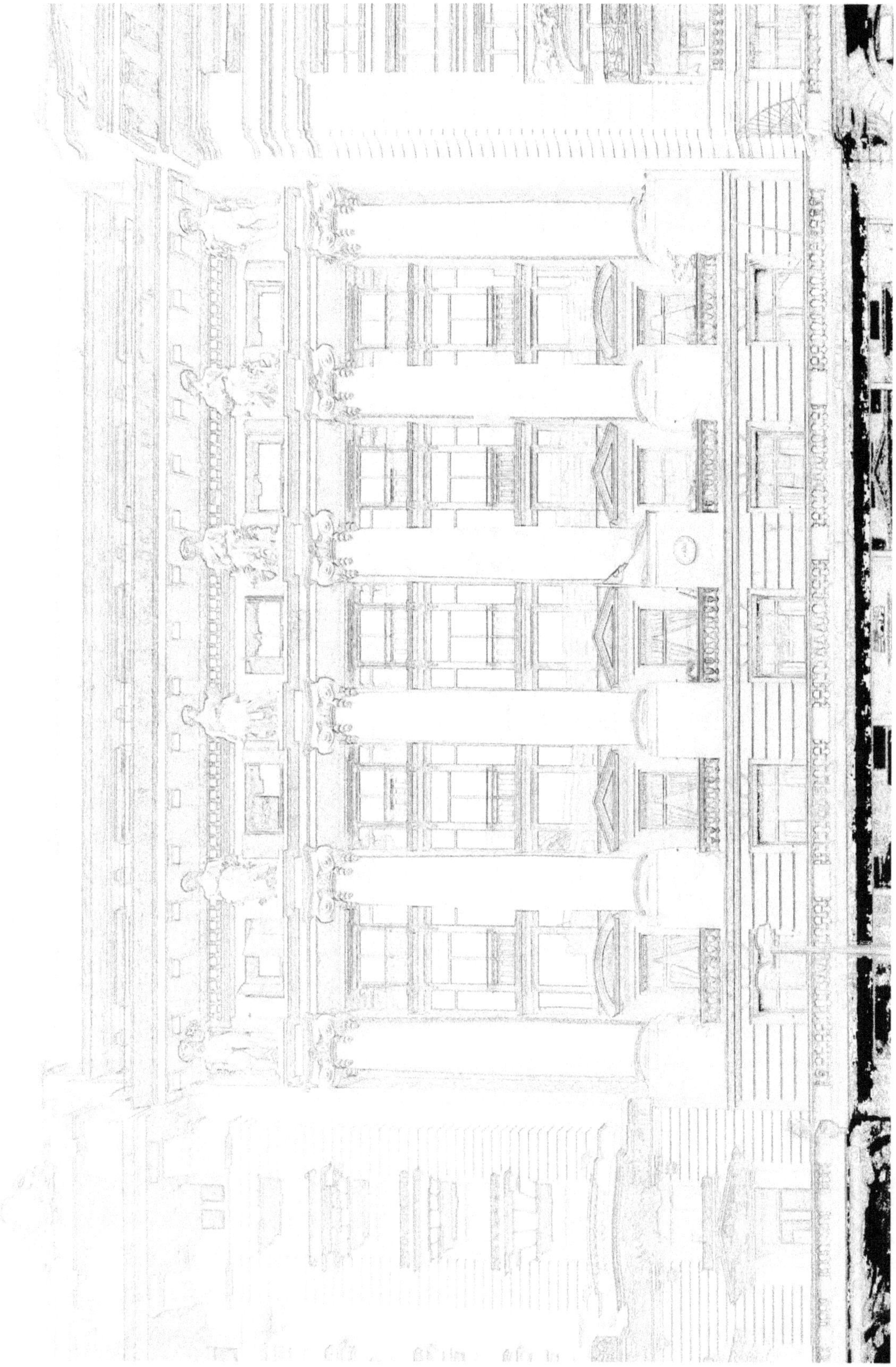

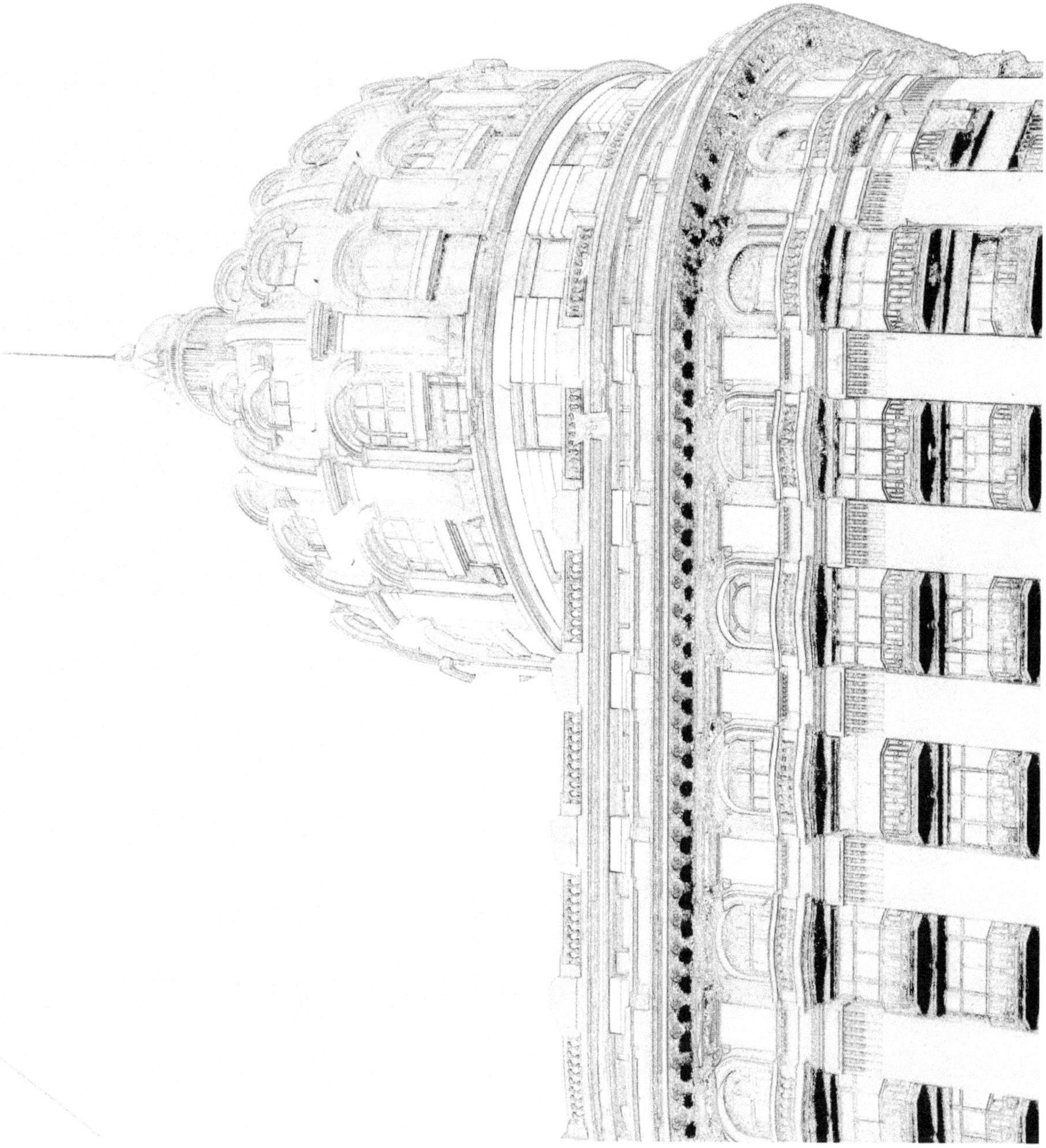

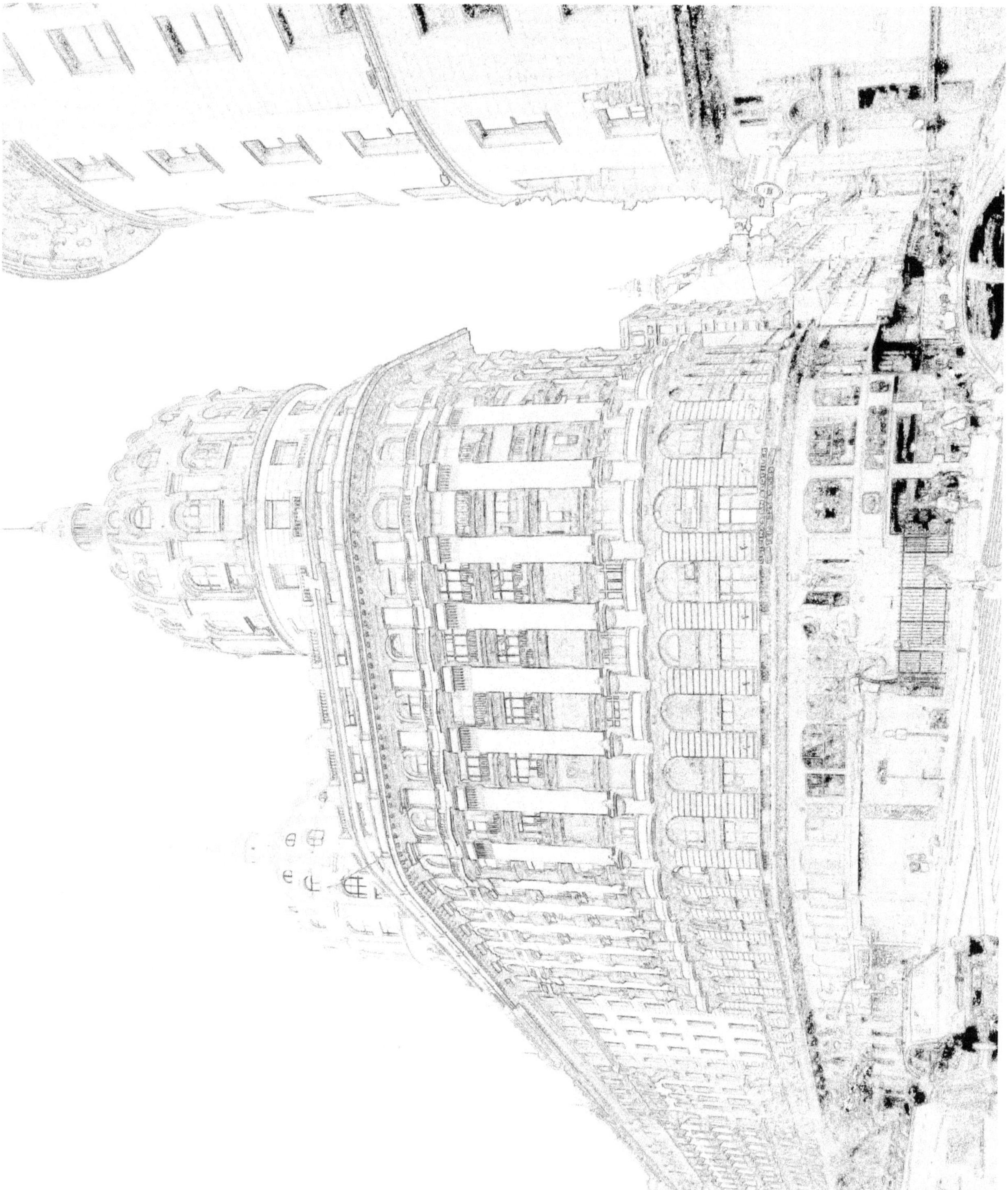

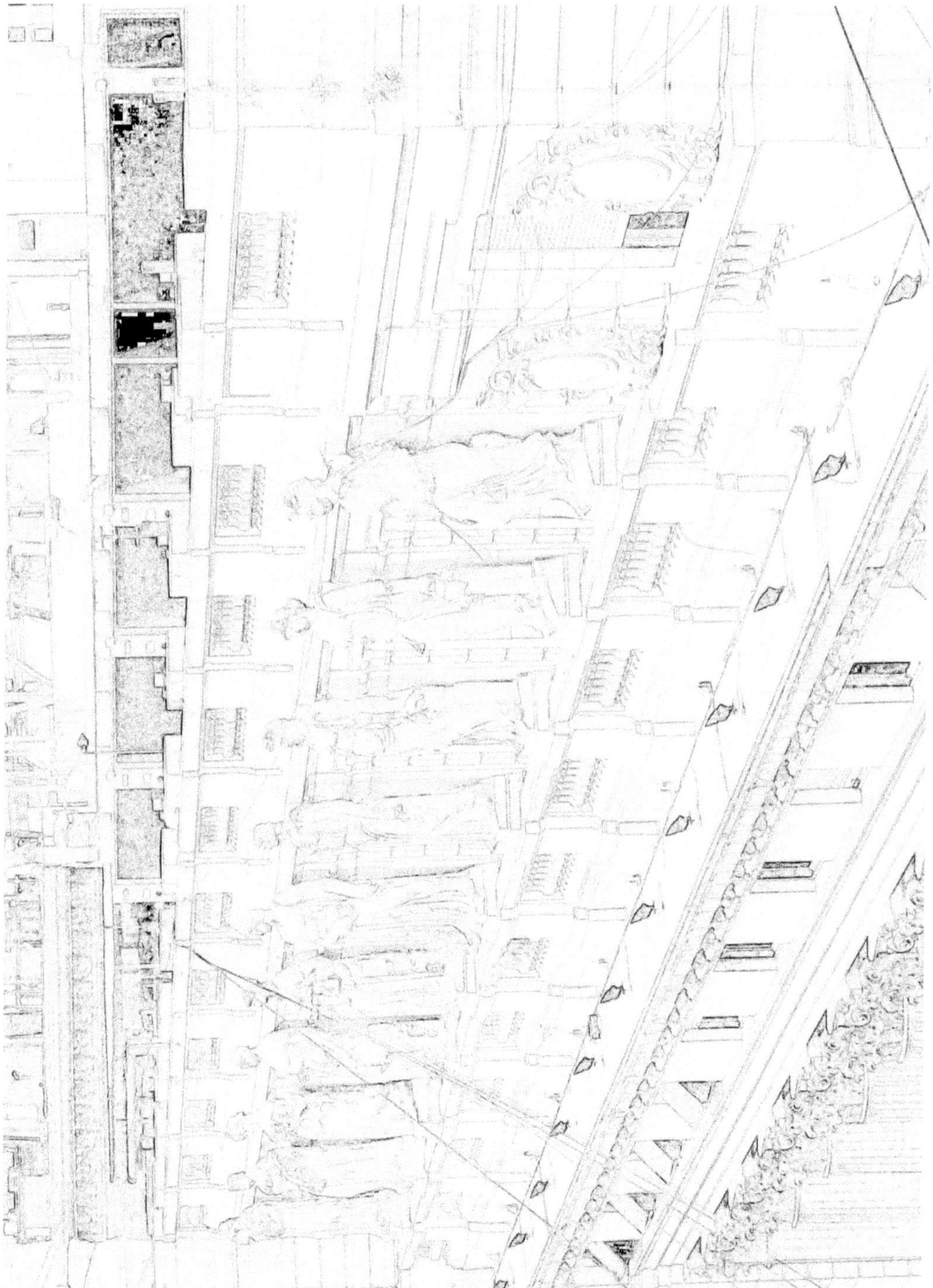

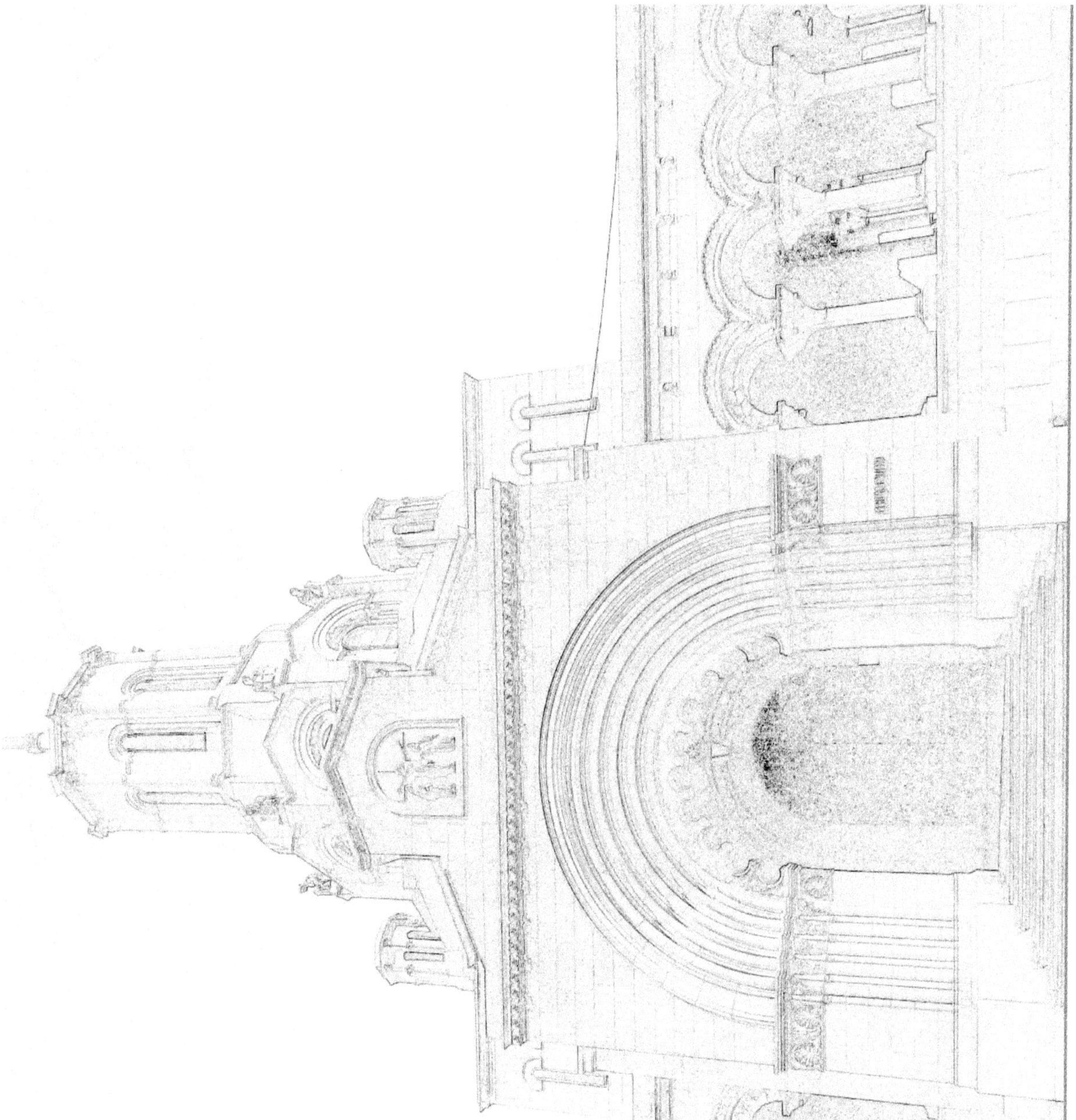

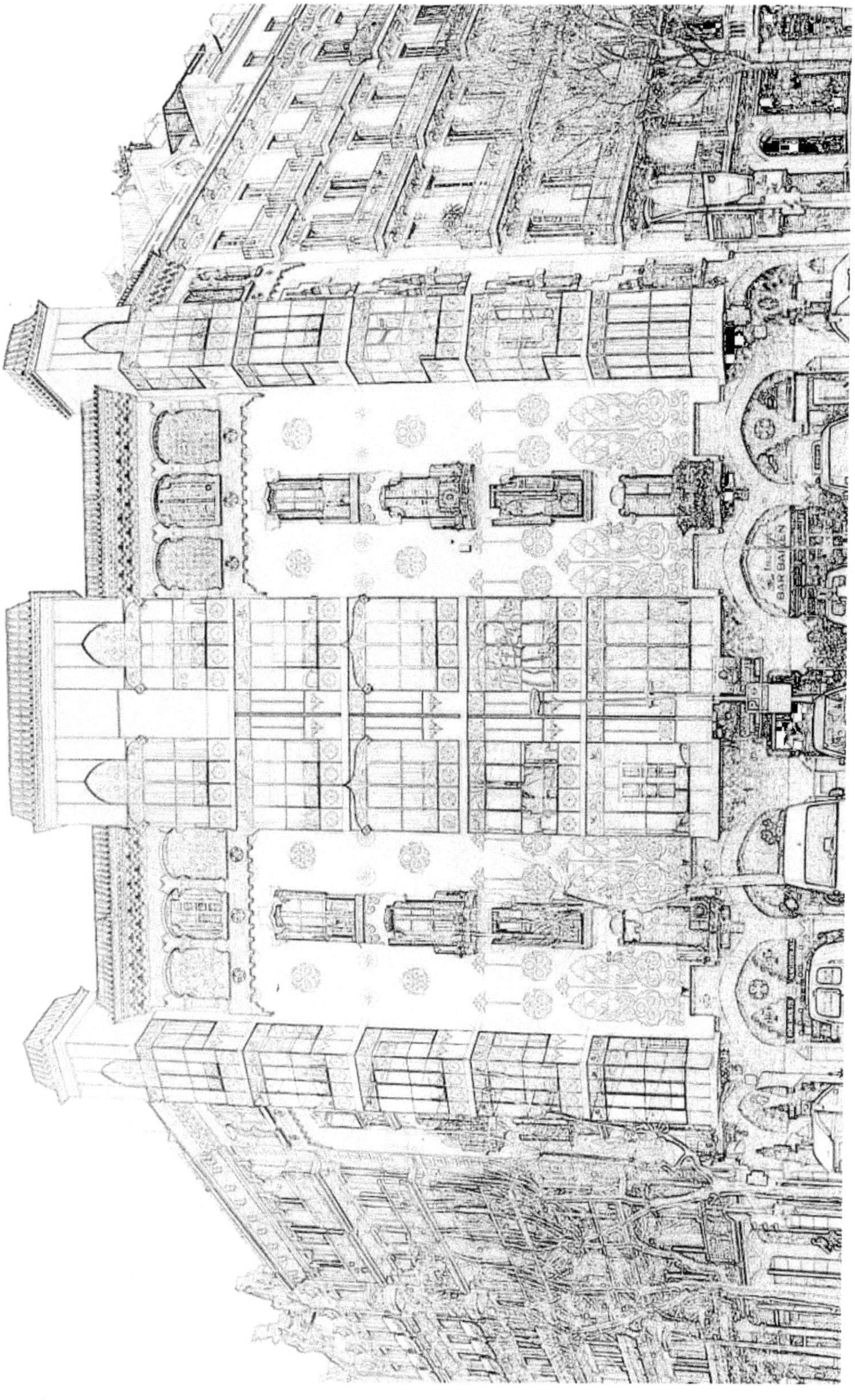

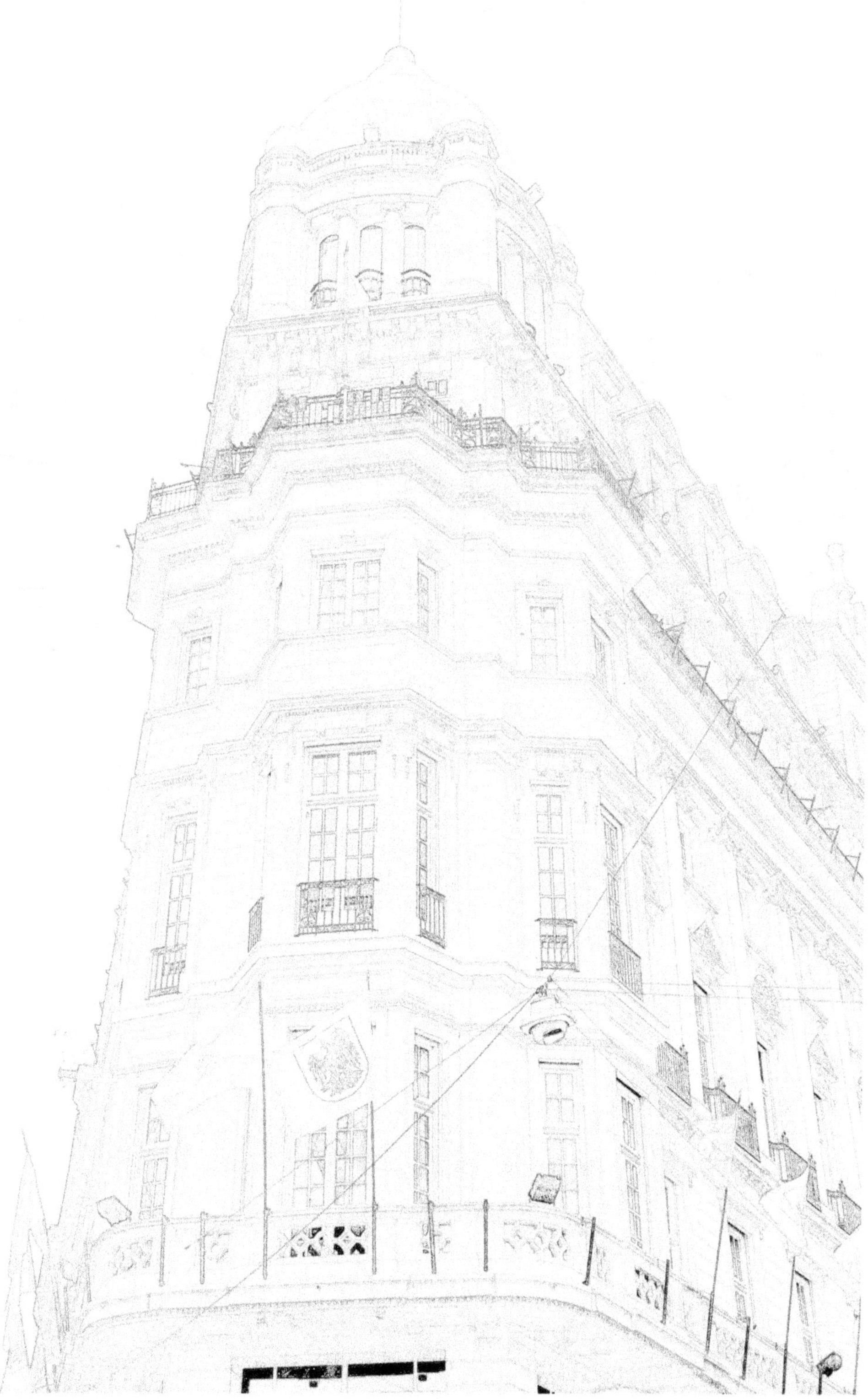

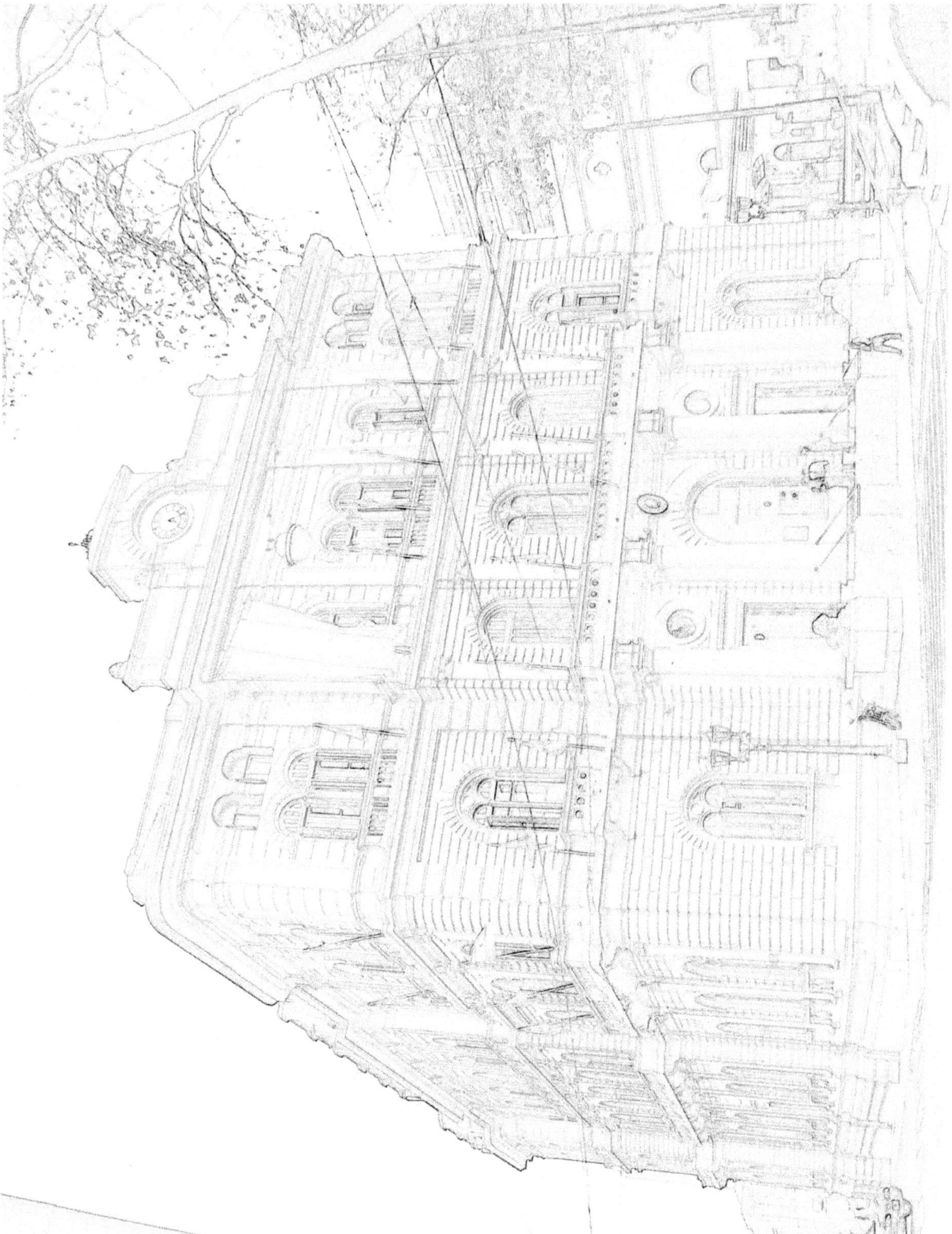

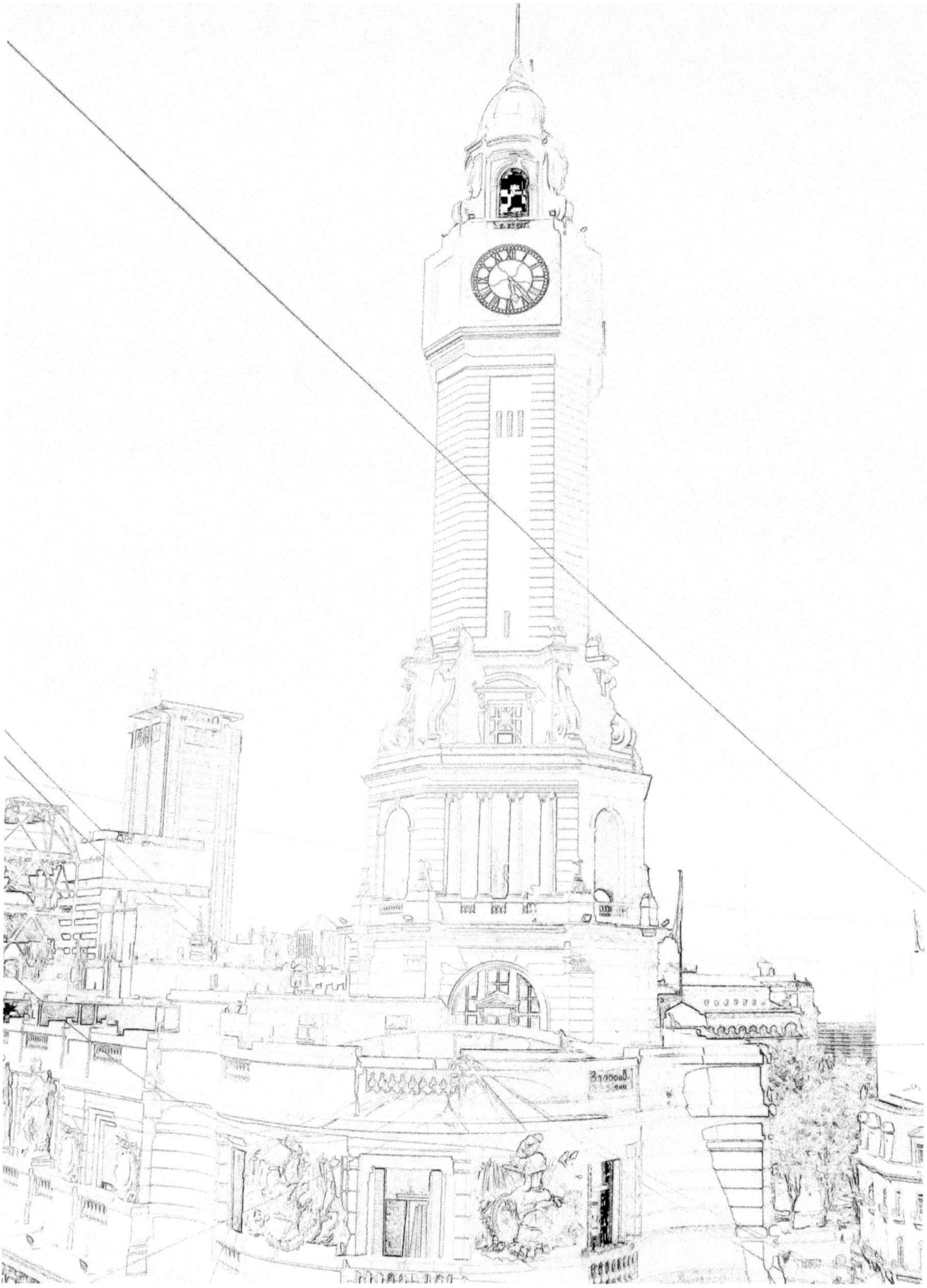

PDF Version this book : http://bit.ly/sketch_12_k

Don't Miss Another our Books.

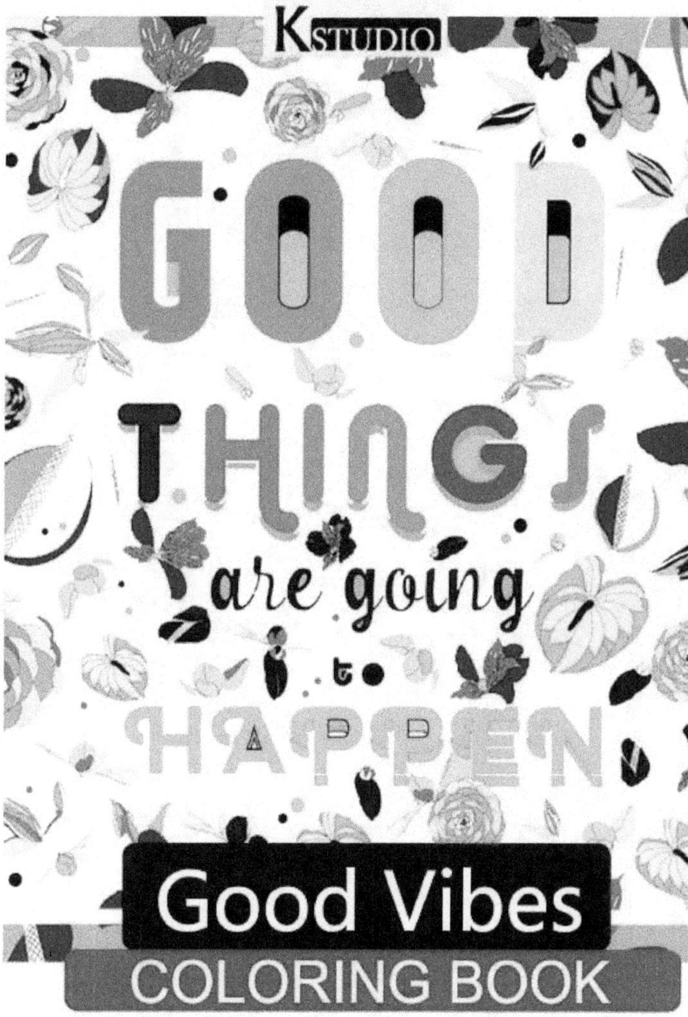

http://bit.ly/good_vibes_1

ISBN : 1530381223

(Use this ISBN for searching on amazon.com)

www.ingramcontent.com/pod-product-compliance
Lightning Source LLC
Chambersburg PA
CBHW080635190526
45169CB00009B/3397
* 9 7 8 1 5 3 6 9 7 7 3 9 4 *